# If You Ho͏
# You Need ͏

**Dolly Mae**

\* **Nameology, the Art and Science of Understanding Names**

# If You Have a Name
# You Need this Book*

### by Dolly Mae

Published by
Sacred Lotus Press
Everett, WA 98204
877 246-9569

**ISBN:** 978-0-9796453-0-3

**Other books by Dolly Mae**
*Choosing Joy in the Midst of Crisis*

To contact the Author or comments, inquiries,
workshops, consultations, and events schedule:
email: dolly@dollymae.com
Web: www.dollymae.com

Cover art: Eric Braff, *ericbraff@mac.com*
Interior design: Tony Stubbs, *www.tjpublish.com*

Printed in the United States
10 9 8 7 6 5 4 3 2

## Acknowledgments and Special Thanks

To my clients the world over,
without whom this book would not be possible.

Their names are all contained herein, letter by letter.

To Patricia Smith and Gail Girard who generously gifted
their time and editing talents.

Eric Braff, an extraordinary, sensitive and creative graphics
artist who makes solutions easy.

# Part I

## WHY THIS BOOK

My goal in writing this book is to give you the tools to uncover the secrets hidden in names. Instead of creating a dictionary of names and their individual meanings, this book shows you how to analyze a name yourself. In unlocking these secrets yourself, you will gain much greater insight into your own personality and others. It is my fervent wish you simply use the tools, guides and examples herein to work out the puzzles in names. You can use it everyday of your life. Remember, if you have a name you need this book!

## What Is Nameology?

Nameology is a blend of numbers, sounds, vibrations, letter shapes and intuition applied to a name revealing hidden information about personality, a life's purpose, its gifts and challenges. While accentuating the values of letters numerically, Nameology gives equal importance to their placements in a name.

## Why Nameology is both Art and Science

The scientific aspect of this knowledge is found in the mathematical study of numbers and the ancient wisdom found within them. This knowledge is expressed through geometry, algebra and calculus and certainly in Da Vinci's famous Vitruvian Man with its perfect geometrical proportions. The ancients understood how numbers and their careful study revealed the interconnectedness of all life.

The Fibonacci number series (1,1,2,3,5,8,13 etc) show us how nature's wisdom and growth factors are scientifically quantifiable. From these insights we may begin to understand our own DNA as well as how repeatable geometric patterns, called fractals, are created.

In this book you will find how nature and the growth of a seed demonstrate the essence of numbers and these patterns.

The artistry of this wisdom is found in the intuitive sciences. This is the practice of applying one's sixth sense to all the knowledge one has acquired. It is not a mystical, no-man's land for the inner few, but a time honored internal wisdom available to all. The simple art of trusting one's inner knowing makes all the difference in the world.

## The Intuitive Art of Nameology

As an intuitive consultant I've used names as my doorway to accessing in-depth information about a client's past, present, gifts, challenges and options ever since I began doing consultations. This information has proven accurate and invaluable. This book is in response to many years of requests to put this information in writing. With the help of this book, you too will soon be able to identify many hidden talents and gifts in names.

## What's in a Name

Our names are fascinating. We hear them tens of thousands of times in our lives. They can be music to our ears or hateful discords. We can change them, shorten them, add to them, take different ones or keep the one we started with. This book will show you why. You will learn how to pick a new name; what a name really means and why a name has deeper meaning.

## Origins

Most names originated from an older language, such as Latin, Greek, Old French, Old English, Teutonic, Germanic, Spanish or Italian. Names originally represented an aspect of one's personality. Dorothy, for instance, has Latin and Greek origins and is derived from 'dor' meaning gift; 'o' meaning of; and 'theo' meaning God, thus Gift of God. Likewise Theodore means the same thing, just in a different order of detail.

As valid and informative as origin information may be, this book is about the meanings that go way beyond these ancient derivations of names.

We will discuss the meanings of names based on a variety of sources such as esoteric information, the hidden and deeper understandings that the ancients used to create names in the first place; and the secret knowledge of the energy of sound and movement that gives rise to the shape of a letter.

We will look at the science of numbers to find numerical values in names that will reveal amazing secrets hidden in plain sight.

We will look at nature to see how this is a natural science reflected in the life all around us.

Finally we will be able to analyze our own names and others' to find the hidden gifts and challenges they offer.

**Packet of Energy**

A name holds a particular packet of energy based on the letters in it and their particular arrangement. Letters are really shapes which have been formed around sound, vibration and energy. Within these letters is a rich tapestry of information about one's personality, gifts and potential. The varied placement of these letters gives an enormous variety of sounds, potentials, challenges and gifts to the many thousands of names. This limited framework of letters held in a single name thus becomes a field of possibilities within which to work and ultimately allow one to break free and experience the extraordinary gifts beyond the confines of that name.

As you hear and speak a vibration many possibilities and potentials open up. You can choose to accept them or reject them. Years of hearing these sounds in your name plus your own personal growth offer you new and unfolding opportunities throughout your life. Thus we grow in our awareness and awakening to enable us to eventually access the most extraordinary of our individual gifts.

## Similarities

Based on thousands of readings, I began noticing similarities and characteristics common among clients' names. Although a general tendency to a characteristic may be common, such as hiding ones emotions; it can manifest in many different ways from total emotional shut down to simply masking one's feelings and pretending.

People were often astounded by the accuracy of details this method revealed about a person. This seemed a natural method to me based on the arrangement of the letters, their sounds and my feelings. Clients asked how it worked.

This book is a guide so you too can learn how it works and how you too can access those secrets in a name. It is a simple process with a few basic rules of understanding. Combining these rules with the ability to sense into the movement, sound and feel of a name and its vibrational tones, will help you access the finer nuances of a name's inner meanings and traits.

**Other Languages**

The method described herein works in any language by using sound and vibration. Some characteristics will change based on different countries and their cultures. This understanding comes with practice. This book however, deals mostly with the English Alphabet.

Even though names and sounds in other languages are different, the principles I will show you still apply. Languages such as Bantu, Hindi, Arabic, Chinese and Japanese use very different sounds, scripts and pictographs. The sounds and vibrations come together so as to create the color and flavor of a language giving rise to individual energy packets of a name.

For the sake of ease, the information herein relates mainly to the first and middle names in the English Alphabet.

**First Names**

Our first names are the ones we are called by and hear over and over. These help give shape to our very nature by their sound, vibration and overtones. The dictionary defines overtones as the almost inaudible higher tones which occur with the fundamental tone. They are the result of the vibration of small sections of a string (instrument) or a column of air. The stringed instrument in this case is the vocal chords with air passing over them.

All of this forms an energy packet that is your personal and distinctive gift. Thus they say no sound is as sweet as the sound of your own name. It is the hand you are dealt at birth for your game of life and is chock full of the 'yet to be experienced'.

You will add to your first name with middle names, nicknames, last names and name changes. These all create new packets of energy to work with, explore and experience. After a name change, it takes between four and seven years to align with the new vibration. If you cannot, you will feel constantly uncomfortable, change your name again, or even get divorced. The new last name will just not blend with you.

People change names when they have major spiritual shifts in their lives. Hence many people who choose spiritual or religious paths may feel the need to take on a new name.

Spirituality and major awakenings shift your focus to a development of the gifts in your name rather than the challenges.

It is interesting to note that most divorces seem to occur at or very close to multiples of 7 (7, 14, 21, 28, or 35) years of marriage. Remember the movie "The Seven Year Itch"? The vibration keeps changing as the partners grow, seeking reintegration with each shift.

## Last Names

The first letter is the most important letter in the last name. For instance, my new last name began with H when I married. H represents structure, organization, responsibility, planning and control on a detailed level. Thus I was able to integrate the work focus of the D of my first name (Dolly) with the organization and structure of the H eventually owning and managing a very large company.

Without that H as the first letter of my last name, the size and growth of the business would have happened differently. My maiden name had an H as its last letter, so the growth and expansiveness of business would have happened, but perhaps in a smaller, less intense way. You see, the first letter is the most important and the others decrease in importance as they occur in the name down to the last letter.

## Like a Game of Cards

Each letter in a name is like a card in the hand we are dealt in a game. Games need rules to give us a finite, manageable field in which to play. The letters, placements, sounds and vibrations make a framework of possibilities, options and opportunities just like the rules of a game. Since names contain only a few letters, they frame the field of possibilities in our game. We then focus on these possibilities to access our gifts and challenges. Changing names expands the game to a bigger field of play.

## Pictures of Energy Movement

It is fascinating to understand that a written letter is actually the picture of how the energy of sound and vibration move. It is actually a diagram. This is specifically true in the Hebrew language and this information has been kept secret in the Ancient mystical teachings of the Jewish Kabala for many centuries. It was only taught to males over age 40, yet we work with it unknowingly every day.

The way the letter is shaped is important in showing how energy flows in and through it and this is much more pronounced in the Hebrew alphabet. In that amazing script, each letter is crafted to show the flow of energy into its physical form.

For instance, the letter R in Hebrew looks like a 7, and is written ר. This is the picture of energy on a higher (spiritual) plane falling to the lower (earth) plane. Resh means head, from which thought flows, and Resh is a symbol for the sun. What a perfect description of solar and spiritual energy in movement.

This is only a sampling of the intriguing depths to which some letters go in reflecting the movement of sound, vibration and energy. Of course, the ancient scripts and alphabets often demonstrate this more clearly than our modern English.

## The Feel of a Letter

It is important to sense into the flow and feel of a letter's energy. Each letter's sound flows over the tongue, lips or back of the throat in a different manner. Just say P, V, S, G, M or L to yourself. Now say their sounds. Instead of Pee or Vee, sound Puh or Vuh. Instead of Ess, sound Sssssss. Instead of Gee, sound Guh. Instead of Em, sound Mmmmmm. Instead of El, sound Luh.

Each one requires creating a different shape with your mouth, lips and tongue. These are the senses, sounds and feelings of a letter. These will be your guide to better understanding each letter and syllable in a name. Look for easy clues like these and feel into a letter.

Take the letter L. Say it over and over. It fairly runs off the tongue like the musical phrase la la la la la. It is open and flows easily. That is the energy of that letter – flowing, graceful, easy movement of sound and vibration. Thus when we find it in a name, we will surely see the person has fluidity and openness in his or her nature as opposed to fixedness.

This is discerned simply from the feel of the letter. Practice how the sound of each letter feels to you.

Note the hardness of K and the softness of M. Note how your breath is exhaled in P. Ultimately, each letter lends a feeling tone to the energy of the name.

The more you look, the more you will find.
The more you listen, the more you will hear.
The more you feel, the more your senses will open up to the wisdom of knowing.

## Full Range of Options

Within each letter's gifts and challenges is a full range of possibilities from totally negative to totally positive. Whether we operate from the highest or lowest possibilities in our name is determined by our genetics, environment, choices, focuses and the spiritual overtone of our lives.

## Identical Names Still Differ

We are complex creatures and we create changes in our world in order to find a way to relate to it. We are all unique. Even though two of us may have the same identical name and there are underlying tendencies that are common; it's how we play our hand of cards that makes the difference. We will each express and experience our names uniquely in this life.

## Soul's Purpose

Originally a name embodied the essence of a soul's purpose. Today most people don't remember they even have a soul's purpose. Thus our name is a way to navigate in our unconscious state until we do awaken and remember that purpose. That is when we will unlock the most astounding gifts our names keep hidden until we are ready.

# Part II

## BASIC RULES AND GUIDELINES

Next you will find the basic rules to begin unraveling the meanings in names. This involves information about Vowels, Consonants, Letter Placement (position) and the Number values of letters.

You will need to combine these ingredients to get a comprehensive picture of a name. Worksheets are provided at the back of the book. Ultimately, with the comfort level that comes with practice, you will make some intuitive leaps and access even deeper meanings in names.

## VOWELS AND CONSONANTS
### Vowels

AEIOU(Y) (and sometimes W; see below)
Note: Y can be both a vowel and a consonant

Vowels represent how emotion is expressed or contained. They denote the level of emotional fluidity. They are the richest part of our being and hold vast and deep keys to personality and how we connect with life through our feelings.

Originally I believe there were seven vowels. The lost vowel was either W (double UU) or a diphthong (blended) sound that we no longer separate out as a distinct vowel, such as ie, ae, eu, or ou. In Canada schools actually used to teach that W was sometimes a vowel. Together these were the sounds of creation; hence the historic sacredness of vowels.

It is interesting to note that it is the differences in pronunciation that often denotes a person's origin. Remember Professor Henry Higgins in 'My Fair Lady' who studied languages. It was specifically the vowel sounds, dropped letters and phraseology that determined a person's class in society. Even today, it is the flattening, accenting, elongating, rounding, nasal quality and clipping of vowels that can reveal the speaker's origins. These are learned behaviors and can be unlearned. James Earl Jones took speech training and now blesses the world with his rich, easily recognizable 'Darth Vader' voice. There is certainly more to it than just the vowels, but they play an invaluable part in the way we hear words and whether or not it is pleasing to our ear.

## Vowels in Ancient Times

In ancient times vowels were never revealed in written languages such as Sanskrit, Hebrew and Egyptian hieroglyphics. Words were written in consonants only. Vowels were considered too powerful to include. Believed to be the holders of our emotional energy, they revealed the hidden, occult and secret power that could touch a person emotionally creating dynamic change. Chanting the vowels could clarify the emotions and align a person's spirit with the Universe and their soul's purpose.

## Number of Vowels in a Name

If there is only one vowel surrounded by consonants in a person's name, feelings are usually hidden or processed internally. The person may be explosive when they finally do let them out. One vowel alone in a name shows internalized emotions. Boiling. Intense. Passionate. Perhaps stuck, but this depends on the sophistication of the person and the other letters.

An excessive number of vowels can make the person hyper, over reactive, highly emotional and dramatic. They need to learn to direct their emotions. They are not in control. At the worst, they could have a split personality.

Of special note is an A as the final letter. These people wear their hearts on their sleeve and are easily hurt. They are also empathic and open to others' feelings.

## The Amazingly Important Vowels and Their Meanings

**A** Independent. Self-aware. Focused.

**E** Versatile. Unsettled. Changeable. Wanderer.

**I** Open-minded. Universal.

**O** Family or community oriented (even extended family to include friends and co-worker). Duty and obligation. Home is needed for balance. Focus on the team.

**U** Sophisticated creativity and expression. Outwardly directed. Universally minded.

**Y** Analytical. Highly spiritual. Consciousness involved in life choices. Sophisticated approach.

## Consonants
## BCDFGHJKLMNPQRSTVWX(Y)Z

Consonants represent how thought is expressed or contained. Although each letter is defined independently, it will be more comprehensive to use both the Nameology Reference Table and the Numbers and Their Meanings sections below to determine the number, meaning and level of each consonant. Combining these pieces of information will be most revealing.

### Balance of vowels and consonants

A balance of vowels and consonants allows a person more balanced emotions and they are able to move more freely between their feelings and thoughts; both those felt internally and those externally expressed.

### Too many consonants

With too few vowels to give them balance, one has perhaps too much emphasis on material things and on making things real and logical in the physical world. They want to know how everything relates to the real world. These people need to sense into their feelings instead of being Mr. Spock and using their intellects to deny, hide from and avoid feelings.

## Consonants and Their Meanings

**B**  Relationship focus, codependency issue.

**C**  Raw creative, artistic energy.

**D**  Work focus, lays a foundation, meets basic needs.

**F**  Family focus, basic issues.

**G**  May seem indecisive, less judgmental.

**H**  Wants to organize, structure and control.

**J**  Has balanced self concept, may be self centered.

**K**  Mastery in life in some way, relationship focus.

**L**  Balanced creative, expressive, artistic energy.

**M**  Work isn't so consuming, changes jobs.

**N**  Change, movement, variety are important.

**P**  Sees both sides of issues, discerning.

**Q**  Organizes structure at a demanding level.

**R**  More global view of life, expansive thinking.

**S**  Sophisticated sense of self.

T   Sophisticated co-dependence, feels gentle.

V   Mastery of details, skilled with people.

W   Cultivated need for change, growth.

X   Unusual and extreme, chaotic energy.

Z   Extreme need for control, disorder.

## BASED ON NUMEROLOGY

Numerology gives each letter a numerical value from 1 to 9 as shown in the following table. Nameology blends numbers, sound, vibration, and intuition. Thus we can base Nameology on this ancient science for part of our understanding.

Nameology is unique in accentuating the values of letters on three different levels (see table) as well as their placements in the name.  In this book we will refer to this table constantly in determining the value and meaning of letters. This is an important key.

## Nameology Reference Table

|         | 1 | 2 | 3 | 4 | 5 | 6 | 7 | 8 | 9 |
|---------|---|---|---|---|---|---|---|---|---|
| Level 1 | A | B | C | D | E | F | G | H | I |
| Level 2 | J | K | L | M | N | O | P | Q | R |
| Level 3 | S | T | U | V | W | X | Y | Z |   |

## THE THREE LEVELS

## First Level ABCDEFGHI

|         | 1 | 2 | 3 | 4 | 5 | 6 | 7 | 8 | 9 |
|---------|---|---|---|---|---|---|---|---|---|
| Level 1 | A | B | C | D | E | F | G | H | I |

These letters are like seed packets of the energies of the numbers 1-9. They hold potential, essence unexpressed and unflowered. Thus they represent the core of undeveloped traits. Elemental. Base. Less refined. More blunt and direct. Ability to cut to the quick. Decisive. Take action, but in a hurried way. Energy is inwardly directed.

## Second Level JKLMNOPQR

|        | 1 | 2 | 3 | 4 | 5 | 6 | 7 | 8 | 9 |
|--------|---|---|---|---|---|---|---|---|---|
| Level 2 | J | K | L | M | N | O | P | Q | R |

These letters represent a more developed and integrated application of the energies of the numbers 1-9. They are more balanced in their vibrations. Each letter is like a flower opening. These are like teenagers in their essence. They are in flux and trying to accomplish and grow. They can see both sides of an issue and can argue for either. Balance of feelings and thought. Balance of doing and being.

## Third Level STUVWXYZ

|        | 1 | 2 | 3 | 4 | 5 | 6 | 7 | 8 | 9 |
|--------|---|---|---|---|---|---|---|---|---|
| Level 3 | S | T | U | V | W | X | Y | Z |   |

This level denotes a sophisticated and more mature application of the energies of the numbers 1-8 (note there are only 8 letters in this level). These energies are socially refined and appropriate in behavior. They may be overly refined and excessive;

exhausting an issue. They see details and clarify them. They are more perceptive. Energy is outwardly directed.

**Memory Key**

Each column of the table has three letters that correspond with a number. This list is a little memory jogger that may help you to easily remember which letters go with which number.

1s  AJS   Remember A Jackass

2s  BKT   Remember Basket

3s  CLU   Remember Clue

4s  DMV  Remember DMV (Dept of Motor Vehicles)

5s  ENW  Remember Entwined

6s  FOX   Remember Fox

7s  GPY   Remember Gypsy

8s  HQZ   Remember Headquarter'z'

9s  IR      Remember IRS (Internal Revenue Service)

## NUMBERS AND THEIR MEANINGS

1. Vibration of independence. Self-contained, like a seed. Self directed. Discernment, but with emotional detachment. Can be obsessive about ideas. Loners. Don't feel connected. Lacking 1s, a person has to master a sense of self in this life. Extremes: egotistical (self-centered); or sensitized to others and doesn't lose ones self (centered in self). Lacking 1s in this life one has to learn self awareness and self-esteem. Career Examples: Idea person. Entrepreneur. Advertising. Think Tank. Inventor. Promoter. Explorer.

2. Group or people oriented. Social. Looking for their values in others. Partnerships. Desire to create and instill harmony and balance with others. More emotional with people. Obsessive. Ascertaining others' feelings. Attention to detail derived from connecting to others. Lacking 2s one has to master relationship and balance in this life. Career Examples: Politician. Secretary. Assistant. Teacher. Electronics. Insurance Adjuster. Accounting. Partnership Law.

3. Creative. Inspirational. Freedom oriented. Don't manipulate me. Need space, don't confine. Intuitive. Artistic. Gut reaction responses. Good common sense. Expansion. Need to become separate through imagination. Creativity. Lacking 3s one has to master communication and creativity in this life. Career Examples: Writer. Artist. Speaker. Author. Baker. Website design. Coach. Music.

4. Strong structure. Needs a base pattern in order to create form and structure. Concerned inwardly and outwardly. Physical elements are important. Work is a focus. Not political at all. Action takers. Job must be done. Independent structure and foundation leading to accomplishment. Adapting. Lacking 4s one has to master health and a sense of the material. Career Examples: Construction. Body Builder. Banker. Business owner. Farmer.

5. Spontaneity. Changeable. Flexibility. Movement. Playfulness. Go. Do. Experience. Adven-

turer. Explorer. Networker. Dancer. Energy in motion. Lacking 5s one has to master play, flexibility and movement in this life, getting unstuck. Career Examples: Travel agent. Military. Acting. Internet. Sales. Communications. Import-Export.

6. Learning and implementing responsibility often through service to others. Associated with home and local community rather than global issues. Very responsible. Know if you don't take care of things, they will fall into ruins. Service to others. Must work with others. Things are established, I can't abandon it; I have to set it in motion. Extremes: codependent, doormats or commitment and obligation phobic. Lacking 6s one has to master service to others in a balanced way in this lifetime. Career Examples: Social worker. Nurse. Doctor. Teacher. Security. Home Repairs. Marriage Counselor. Interior Decorator. Landscaper. Hairdresser. Fashion.

7. Analytical. Looking for the hidden, the unknowable. Seeing both sides of issues. Discerning. Objective view. Offer suggestions for improvement, but they don't always follow through. Analysts. Editors. Reviewers. Clarifiers. Determines need for organizing, expansion, direction. The processor. The thinker. Extremes: Cynical. Sarcastic. Critical or Genius with insight. Lacking 7s one has to master balancing of concepts, openness, secretiveness and objectivity. Career Examples: Priest. Counselor. Advice columnist. Negotiator. Arbitration. Attorney. Scientist. Researcher.

8. Ability to apply and stabilize the energy and issues of double 4s (creating form) and 2s (balance in relationships). Interacts with others in sophisticated way. Delegates. Motivates. Administrates. Organizes. Pulls it all together. Synergizing successfully. Management expertise. Social. Patriotic. Lacking 8s one needs to master organizing, detail work and finances in this life. Career Examples:

Administrator. Principal. Big Business owner. Finance. Management. Supervisor, Project director. Banking. Engineer. Business Law. Real Estate. Investigator. Forensics.

9    Unlimitedness.  Expansive in concepts and creativity. Not having to be caught in the details. Universality. No desire for pettiness or nonsense. Open-minded. Global concern. Has many completions and endings in this lifetime, often in 9 year increments. Opens up inwardly to the universe. Lacking 9s one has to master open-mindedness, universal thinking, timely conclusions of relationships and situations. Career Examples: International Business. Spiritual Healer. Magician. Diplomat. Surgeon. Universal Teacher.

Master numbers: 11 & 22 are not reduced in numerology to 2 and 4, as they represent the higher octaves of vibration than simpler 2s and 4s. They give sophistication to the vibration of 2, can create sophisticated, chaotic lives full of trauma. They work on testing their strengths. They are applying lessons learned.

The following two letters in any name, K and V always indicate achievement of mastery on some level in this life. It could be career, spirituality, relationships or intellectually. Names with K or V are usually endlessly fascinating people with untapped depths.

11 is K, the 11th letter of the alphabet.

Mastery in the world of creating inspired peace (the higher vibration of 2). Their work is inspired with a Divine insight. The Cosmic view. Inspired creativity.

Career Examples: Motivational writer. Inspirational speaker. Metaphysician. Astronaut. Sales Manager. Leader.

22  is V, the 22nd letter of the alphabet

Mastery in the world of form (the higher vibration of 4). Superb manifesting in the physical world. Career Examples:  Executive level government. Humanitarian. Schools. Mediation. Diplomat.

## Numbers Summary

1  Self Awareness, Unfolded potential.

2  Relationship focus, Seeks balance.

3  Creative, Artistic, Expressive.

4  Needs structure, Work focus.

5  Change, Travel, Play, Movement.

6  Service to others, Community focus.

7  Sees both sides of issues, Objective.

8  Organize, Control, Management, Money.

9  Brings to completion, Open minded, Universal.

11 Divine insight & creativity, Mastery of inspiration.

22  Mastery in business, Humanitarian.

## Let Nature Be Our Guide

Nature is our master teacher. From her we are able to derive all wisdom that exists on this plane of learning. The plants which taught us the Fibonacci numbers and the geometrical precision of fractals are keys to the secrets of our own DNA. Whatever we need to know, we may seek understanding in observing Nature.

By examining a plant's growth, we may relate to abstract numbers in a richer and earthier way. This exercise in visualizing the mystery and miracle of a seed's growth is a perfect analogy for understanding numbers.

Imagine a seed (this is the number 1). It is whole, complete, yet unexpressed. All essence is contained within.

As it divides it becomes 2, entering into partnership with new aspects of itself.

As it begins to put out shoots, it becomes 3, the result of the birthing experience. This is male and female producing offspring; and the tension of duality being resolved in trinity.

Roots begin to embrace the earth expressing the groundedness of the number 4. Roots give the plant stability.

The branches grow, seeking movement and expression which is the number 5. Varying in their movement, they create expansion.

The plant requires nurturing, must be watered and fed, taken care of. This expresses the number 6, service to other (the plant).

As the plant grows, it must be cultivated, weeded, trimmed, pruned and shaped. Determining just the right way is the art of the 7, balancing and enhancing its growth through discernment.

With the 8 we harvest the crop produced by our nurtured plant. We reap the benefits of the seed splitting, the care and feeding and of the overall details of supervision.

The 9 is the rest after the harvest. It is a time of lying fallow, internal nurturing, simply being instead of doing. The 9 can reflect on the larger picture of the plant's place in the game of life. It has done its work and provided fruit. It will begin its internal process once more in the appropriate season at a newer and richer level.

Thus each series of numbers 1-9 finds a level of completion, but never a conclusion. Always the next series reveal a higher level of themselves. In numbers 10-19 we add each of the numbers together. Thus the 10 (1 + 0) is merely a 1, the 11 (1 + 1) is a 2 although it is also a master number, the 12 (1 + 2) is a 3 and so on. Each level displays a higher vibration of growth, on and on, endlessly.

So too do we. There is truly no end to our growth, just a new cycle, a new level of movement and progression and learning and experiencing. We may choose to resist or embrace each new level of growth. It is always and forever a choice.

## Summary

1. Seed
2. Seed dividing
3. Germination of shoots
4. Putting down roots
5. Branching
6. Gardening process, watering, feeding, fertilizer
7. Weeding and Pruning
8. Harvest
9. Fallow, rest, waiting for next season of growth

## Part III

## PLACEMENT OF LETTERS

It is of great importance where a letter falls in a name. There seems to be more significance in the placement of the letters than in the letters themselves. I will first explain what position means. Later we will put it all together, position, numerical value and level (using the Table).

Remember, we are focusing on first names here.

### First Letter Importance

This letter gives us our main direction, emphasis, and focus in our lifetime. It represents how a person is internally within her soul, but hasn't yet learned to present externally. When they do express how they are inside, they will have matured a great deal.

Using Dolly as an example, look up D in the Nameology Reference Table. It is a 4 on Level 1. Look up number 4 and note what it means. Combine this with what it means to be on the first level. Thus we learn what D from Dolly means: Internally, she wants to accomplish, create order and to have a career. Externally she is constantly striving to accomplish. She is hard working or perhaps needs to create a work focus and may often be unemployed. If the first letter is a vowel, emotions will predominate in an individual's life and the person may often lose control.

**Second Letter:**

If a vowel, it will express your emotional direction or sensitivity. (See Amazingly Important Vowels above.)

If a consonant, it intensifies the need to accomplish the meaning of the letter and gives a sense of deliberateness, of obligation and necessity. (e.g. If a C, which is a 3 on Level 1, then it intensifies the need to create and express its potential.)

## The First Vowel

This tells us the emotional sense of the person, their fluidity in feeling and sensing their environment.

## Center Letter(s), the Pivot

This will be one letter in names with an odd number of letters and two letters in a name with an even number of letters, e.g. Dolly has an odd number, hence only one pivot, the letter L. Patricia has an even number, hence two pivot letters: R and I. The pivot letter(s) show how the person interacts with others to be able to fulfill their life's purpose. It shows how they make changes and learn to change in their lives to best express their gifts. The pivot is what they need to change or how to change. The secrets of the pivot letters give clues as to how one can get unstuck in their path and redirect their energy towards accomplishment of their life's purpose. The letters on either side of this pivot give insight into how that person opens up and helps others.

**Examples and their meanings:**

E as the pivot letter. (Greta) One needs to be more playful, imaginative and open to change and the variable options for solution.

O as pivot letter. (Scott) One needs to look at the responsibility of home as having as much value as a profession.

L as pivot letter. (Sally) One needs to be creative and expressive.

The pivot letter is similar to the North Node in Astrology. The North Node guides us to our life's purpose, away from old patterns of stuckness from past experiences or past lives.

## Letters on Both Sides of the Pivot

These letters show how you influence others and the ways you use your talents to interact with them.

## Examples and their meanings:

T and C in Patricia. These are the two letters found beside the pivot letters R and I. Thus Patricia influences others and interacts with them in sophisticated partnership working on keeping them in balance (the T); and by working with her elemental sense of creativity and communication to interact with others (the C).

O and L in Dolly, surrounding the pivotal L. The O shows she influences others by valuing them as extended family in an evenhanded way; while the L shows she uses her balanced communication skills to interact.

## First Consonant After the First Letter

This letter gives an idea of the person's career possibilities (see Numbers and their Meanings above).

**Examples and their meanings:**

Brian, Dorothy or Arlene: The R means wanting to be more universal, working for the whole, wanting to travel more and to think expansively.

Dean: The N means wanting to be more playful and create change. Though in a short name and as the last letter, it has additional meanings.

**Last Letter of First Name**

At the end of a first name, an A, J or S means that the person will up-level themselves in this lifetime, emotionally, mentally and spiritually, thus feeling they have lived more than one lifetime in this life. If they are stubborn about change, they may be more inclined to Alzheimer's or even brain injury. If it's an A, they probably have to have the last word and they attempt to be clear in their statements. As mentioned before, their feelings are easily hurt and they are empathic.

If this last letter is a consonant, as in Dean, the person tends not to be empathic but to use thought to maintain a sense of identity, enabling them to separate themselves from others easily.

## Letters of Note

Th anywhere in a name often denotes the power behind the throne. These people support another's power and are either manipulative or become a victim of that person. They will organize and manage things for someone they feel subordinate to someone they feel is their superior, e.g. Theodore, Dorothy, or Cathy.

An ie at the end of a first name indicates a diminutive. Often there is a sense of being less than others, feeling smaller, perhaps not as good as, or being a favorite or pet. Men rarely keep the ie of their childhood names, such as Jimmie, Donnie, or Frankie. They would consider it too childish or immature. Cutting off the ie lets them grow up. On the other hand, women often keep the ie as in Julie, Katie, Jeannie.

## DOUBLE LETTERS

### Double Consonants

These denote obsessive, compulsive behavior. In Dolly the double ll indicates obsessive, compulsive need for freedom, expansiveness, independence, creativity and intuition. This is the energy of the number 3. Usually sophisticated, but obsessive and compulsive if not spiritually directed.

Double tt indicates codependency issues, due to a compulsive need for social interaction, which is the energy of the number 2.

### Double Vowels

Double vowels such as ee, oo, aa, ii indicate these individuals tend to be emotionally exaggerated. They may have wild emotional swings or be emotionally self-indulgent. Extremes: may have behavioral or psychological issues. Fireworks anger. Deep depression, possible use of drugs or chemical dependency.

If a person has spirituality as a focus, they can use the compulsiveness of double letters to direct these powerful energies in a positive way, like a charioteer with wild horses. They may use this intensity to deepen the gifts of their name and of their connection with the Divinity.

## The Letter Y

Y can actually be either a vowel or a consonant, though I favor using it as a vowel. With this letter, an individual may choose to be harder or softer in nature. It gives them a choice. It lets the individual consciously direct their energy, like that team of horses, controlled or not. In either case their life will have a spiritual or religious focus.

## Capital Letters in the Middle of the Name as in JoAnn or DuWayne

This makes a compound of first letters, so you will have two important first letters in such a name. The A acts like another first letter and in this case it's a vowel giving it even more importance.

## Middle Name as Modifier

The middle name modifies and adds to the energies and potentials of the first name. However if it has become the first name by usage, then treat your 'real' first name as a middle name. All of its letters are important, but its first letter has the greatest value. All the same methods apply as with the first name, but with somewhat less importance. There will be greater importance if the middle name is used regularly with the first name as in Mary Ellen, Jo Beth or Billy Bob.

## The Final Touch

The final touch in understanding a name is the intuitive or psychic leap to an overall synthesis and super-understanding of a name. This includes an overriding knowing of the distinguishing aspects of how a particular person utilizes the gifts and challenges of their name. This is the ability to put all the puzzle parts together in a cohesive picture to give an accurate impression of the energy packet of a name. Practice will bring great satisfaction to you. Learn to trust your intuition and you will feel more comfortable in your assessments.

# Part IV

## HOW IT WORKS

Begin by first viewing the name as a whole. Pay particular attention to the first letter, the final letter and any double letters. Note special letters such as k, v, ie, or th.

Then begin to work with each letter determining details regarding numerical value and level by using the Nameology Reference Table. For instance an L is numerically a 3 on Level 2. Refer to the previous text in this book about the Number 3 and Level 2. Combining this information will immediately reveal many surprising clues. You may wish to use the Vowel and Consonant Summary Lists as shortcuts.

Next, look to the placement of the letter and determine what additional information can be gleaned.

Note whether the vowels are hemmed in by consonants or are open, as in first and final letters.

You will need to refer to many sections of this book at first until you become familiar with the concepts.

Review the examples here and then use the worksheets at the back of the book to reveal what's in your own name.

**Two Names Explained in Detail**

In the following paragraphs we will see just how this works when applied to two famous names: Yeshua and Bill Gates. The Nameology Reference Table is repeated here for your convenience.

## Nameology Reference Table

|  | 1 | 2 | 3 | 4 | 5 | 6 | 7 | 8 | 9 |
|---|---|---|---|---|---|---|---|---|---|
| Level 1 | A | B | C | D | E | F | G | H | I |
| Level 2 | J | K | L | M | N | O | P | Q | R |
| Level 3 | S | T | U | V | W | X | Y | Z | |

## Yeshua

First letter Y is a 7 (remember GYPsy) on Level 3, the sophisticated level.

The all important first letter Y shows a Spiritual Focus. It's both vowel and consonant, so there's an initial grand balance mentally and emotionally. This is consciously directed energy. A decision was made in his case to focus his spirituality.

First vowel E is a 5 on Level 1. This is the emotional ability of change and flexibility, showing people how to adapt, change and play.

Pivot letters are SH (Yeshua).

The S is a 1 on Level 3.

The H is an 8 on Level 1.

These pivot letters show how he fulfills his life's purpose, how he will make changes in his life and what he needs to change. This will be done through a sophisticated sense of self, the S of Level 3, combined with a need to organize and structure events and things on a grand scale, this is the organizational ability of the H.

The H shows an ability to interact with others in an organized and sophisticated way. He can pull it all together synergistically and needs to direct others in a focused way.

Letters on both sides of the pivot letters are E & U.
E is a 5 on Level 1.
U is a 3 on Level 3.
This is how he interacts with others. E reflects his ability to create and express change and flexibility; in this case spiritually, in thought and feeling. U tells us of his need to spark and awaken the sophisticated creative force within others. Thus he makes a good teacher.

A as the last letter is a 1 on Level 1. It shows us he is empathic and open to others' feelings and that he has a complex sense of self-awareness.

If we look at what numbers are missing, we find no 2, 4 or 6. However, we find an 8, which is a higher vibration of, and includes 2 and 4 energy. The missing 6 is what he came in to do: service to others.

## Bill Gates (Born William Henry Gates III)

There just had to be an 8 in his name, the H meaning huge structure in business; and the I is a prominent 9, indicating his Global view.

First letter B is a 2 on Level 1. So we know a focus for him in this lifetime is partnerships and relationships, both business and personal. He has a need to define and balance in all basic experiences.
The first Vowel I is a 9 on Level 1. This is his huge, intensely packed global perspective.

The double LL are 3s on Level 2. They show his compulsive need for freedom and independence, especially in his creative direction.

The fact there is only one vowel in Bill shows us he is not truly available to his feelings and that he shelters them amidst consonants representing thinking. He feels safer in his intellectual world and expresses most of his feelings intellectually.

With very common names like Bill, we look to the second name for additional information, to clarify and expand the particulars of the first.

Thus, the H of his second name Henry gives us a gigantic clue as to his 'aholic' behavior: big business, expansive structure and organization. Coupled with the two Is in his name, this give us a clue about his global consciousness and its need for expression in his life.
Note the lack of 4s in Bill Gates' name. The prominent 8, the H, incorporates the lower vibrational 4 meaning work and the creation of form. The 8

means work on a grander scale and larger concept of form and structure which certainly represents Mr Gates.

**Shortcuts**

In years of research, I have found certain names to have consistent behavior patterns.

**Addictions**

Bills are 'aholics' meaning they have compulsive patterns of conduct, like an addiction. Please understand that by addiction I mean something to which a person has given away his power and hence to which he is bound. There may even be more than one at a time.

This may be as regards work, sex, drugs, alcohol, possessions, religion, relationships, money or food. Somehow the compulsive, addictive nature will be expressed. In Gates' case, it is certainly work. Extremes in conduct, appropriateness, spiritual awareness, and other factors determine the value of the addiction as positive or negative. Hence we may view this Bill's workaholic patterns and commitment as tremendously positive in its effect on billions of lives.

It was no accident that the recovering alcoholic who started Alcoholics Anonymous was named Bill W. We are endlessly amazing and varied creatures. Thus we see addiction is neither bad nor good, but how it is applied that determines its value.

To discover which addictive nature a particular Bill has, we must rely on intuition and perhaps a middle name with its additional, modifying energy. Then again, it may be none of our business and we should leave it to the individual's discretion.

## Psychics and Intuitives

These names always indicate great psychic ability, whether actually being used or not. Usually these people are aware of their intuitive gifts. Isabelle, Irene,

Lynn, Dorothy, Dolly, Charles, Richard, Claire, Clarissa, and Dolores. This is by no means a complete list, just some of the most common names.

There are names that indicate victims, names that indicate sexual abuse and names that indicate other unusual tendencies and practices. As you work with this information and apply it, you will begin to form your own dictionary of names and their specific and unusual peculiarities. They will stand out.

Many common names of old are unused today such as Dorothy, Ruth, Constantine. This is a good thing. The old energies are leaving. New names, new energies and new combinations of letters are being birthed to allow for a new vibration of human to come in to this planet.

Indigo, Crystal and Rainbow children are the next generation of genetics on this planet. They will break the old bonds, limitations and patterns of names and create new ones for themselves. Thus we are seeing different names for children nowdays such as Cole, Jade, and Brandon. Yes, we can point to Cole Porter and say it's an old name, but the creativity it represented is reborn with new dynamics in these new children. Expect great things from them. They will astound us.

# Part V

## CREATING A NAME

### Nicknames

If we create a nickname for a friend, it is because intuitively the vibration of their name doesn't seem to fit. We pick one that feels more like them and creates a more comfortable, compatible bridge between us.

If you wish to create a new name for yourself, use the guidelines you find in this book. Remember it will take approximately four years to integrate and align with this new name's vibration.

## Naming Babies

When naming children we often use the name of a relative or friend to honor them or carry on the tradition. Other times we choose a favorite name from literature. Certainly we are gifting the child with the qualities we like in that other person. We may also be gifting them with similar life challenges.

## Baby Naming Ceremonies

Numerous cultures recognize the importance of the gifts a name bestows on a child. The naming ceremony imbues the child with the gifts offered in the name's energy packet. Thus a highly ritualized naming ceremony often takes place soon after birth. This is a traditional celebration of acknowledgement and acceptance of the infant by the community. It is also a symbol of the infant's entry into its own new experience as a member of humanity. The naming of a child has great importance everywhere. There seems to be an innate knowing that the name carries enormous meaning and potential.

## Hints on How to Name a Child

If you want your child to be open to feelings, begin their name with a vowel.

If you want your child to be empathic, end their first name with a vowel, especially an A.

If you want your child to have the best chance of balance with emotion and reason, have equal numbers of vowels and consonants.

If you want creativity, use C, L or U prominently (first, second or middle letter of first name).

If you want spirituality to be important in their lives, include a Y.

If you want closeness in family try an F or an O.

If you want them to be more of a mediator and to see both sides of issues, try a G, P or Y.

Study all the other tools herein and choose what feels best.

Remember you are not molding this little soul to be exactly what you want by choosing and placing letters, but you are giving them certain options and opportunities. How they choose to express them is their choice. For instance, you may want them to be an artist, so you use all the most creative letters, C, L and U, and little 'Claude' ends up a graffiti expert on the freeway underpass, jailed for vandalism! How we express our abilities is based on our self worth, woundedness, fears and sense of love. The name is the hand of cards we are dealt. How we play them out in life is up to us.

Even the most challenging names have among them those who have gone down in history and changed our lives. We have already mentioned the extraordinary 'aholics' Bill W., founder of AA, and Bill Gates. How about Aaron, Moses' brother with those challenging double aa's? He made history by focusing that passionate and intense energy. What about Elizabeth with that subordinating th; a Queen with regal power, she subordinated herself to her country and its people.

So don't worry about challenges. They are there to rise above and ultimately they can become our greatest gifts. Once we step onto a spiritual or religious path, those gifts become even more dominant.

**Mistakes**

There aren't any! You do the best you can in each moment.

No matter what your child's birth name, it was and is not a mistake! You gave them the gift of life in this reality. Your offer of love throughout their lives supports them in the best possible way. So don't worry about the past or the future. Your child gets to choose, create and reinvent him or herself throughout his or her whole lifetime, just like you do! In truth, their spirit helped you create their name way before their physical appearance in this world.

## In Conclusion

Every name, no matter what it offers has a famous person who has worn it proudly. Remember, everything is just an indicator, not written in stone. You are the creator of your life.

Play with names and work out their meanings. You now have the tools to discover the secrets in every name and you will be amazed. My hope is you have loads of fun with this intriguing game and you play often.

Most of all have fun!

## ADDENDUM:

## WORKSHEETS FOR YOUR NAME

Additional worksheets available at *www.dollymae.com*

On the next several pages are worksheets that will unlock the secrets of each letter of your name.

Each page is for one letter. As you work, make notes of the words and meanings from the text in this book that apply to each letter. At the end, your written notes will read like a story of the name, full of information and detail.

Use this handy table repeated here for ease of reference.

### Nameology Reference Table

|         | 1 | 2 | 3 | 4 | 5 | 6 | 7 | 8 | 9 |
|---------|---|---|---|---|---|---|---|---|---|
| Level 1 | A | B | C | D | E | F | G | H | I |
| Level 2 | J | K | L | M | N | O | P | Q | R |
| Level 3 | S | T | U | V | W | X | Y | Z |   |

FIRST NAME _____
(Use the name you are called by)

Number of Vowels ____ Consonants ____ (p. 27)

Are vowels closed in or on the ends? Meaning: (p. 25)

First Letter _____ (p. 44) Vowel    Consonant
(Circle One)

Letter Meaning (p. 26-29)

Numerical value    1 2 3 4 5 6 7 8 9    (p. 30)
Circle One)

Which Level is it? First / Second / Third (p. 30)
(Circle one)

Notes on the Numerical value: (p. 33-39)

Notes on the Level: (p. 30-31)

Notes on the Position: (p. 44-50)

Second Letter ____ (p. 45) Vowel or Consonant
(Circle One)

Letter Meaning (p. 26-29)

Numerical value   1 2 3 4 5 6 7 8 9  (p. 30)
(Circle One)

Which Level is it?  First / Second / Third    (p. 30)
(Circle one)

Notes on the Numerical value: (p. 33-39)

Notes on the Level:  (p. 30-31)

Notes on the Position: (p. 44-50)

If this is the last letter in your name, skip to Final Letter page.

Is this the First CONSONANT after the first letter? Then it shows career possibilities based on what number the letter is in the table. Write down some of these that feel right for you. (p. 33-39)

Third Letter _____ (p. 45)    Vowel or Consonant
(Circle One)

Letter Meaning (p. 26-29)

Numerical value    1 2 3 4 5 6 7 8 9    (p. 30)
(Circle One)

Which Level is it?  First / Second / Third    (p. 30)
(Circle one)

Notes on the Numerical value:  (p. 33-39)

Notes on the Level:  (p. 30-31)

Notes on the Position:  (p. 44-50)

If this is the last letter in your name, skip to Final Letter page.

Is this the First CONSONANT after the first letter? Then it shows career possibilities based on what number the letter is in the table. Write down some of these that feel right for you. (p. 33-39)

Fourth Letter \_\_\_\_\_ (p. 45)  Vowel or Consonant
(Circle One)

Letter Meaning (p. 26-29)

Numerical value  1 2 3 4 5 6 7 8 9  (p. 30)
(Circle One)

Which Level is it?  First / Second / Third  (p. 30)
(Circle one)

Notes on the Numerical value:  (p. 33-39)

Notes on the Level:  (p. 30-31)

Notes on the Position:  (p. 44-50)

If this is the last letter in your name, skip to Final Letter page.

Is this the First CONSONANT after the first letter?. Then it shows career possibilities based on what number the letter is in the table. Write down some of these that feel right for you. (p. 33-39)

Fifth Letter _____ (p. 45)     Vowel or Consonant
                                    (Circle One)

Letter Meaning (p. 26-29)

Numerical value    1 2 3 4 5 6 7 8 9   (p. 30)
                        (Circle One)

Which Level is it?  First / Second / Third  (p. 30)
                          (Circle one)

Notes on the Numerical value:  (p. 33-39)

Notes on the Level:  (p. 30-31)

Notes on the Position:  (p. 44-50)

If this is the last letter in your name, skip to Final Letter page.

Sixth Letter _____ (p. 45)     Vowel or Consonant

(Circle One)

Letter Meaning (p. 26-29)

Numerical value   1 2 3 4 5 6 7 8 9   (p. 30)
(Circle One)

Which Level is it?  First / Second / Third  (p. 30)
(Circle one)

Notes on the Numerical value:  (p. 33-39)

Notes on the Level:  (p. 30-31)

Notes on the Position:  (p. 44-50)
If this is the last letter in your name, skip to Final Letter page.

Final Letter _____ (p. 49)    Vowel or Consonant
(Circle one)

See "Last letter of First Name" to understand the meaning of vowel vs consonant here.  Make notes that apply to you.

Letter Meaning (p. 26-29)

Numerical value    1 2 3 4 5 6 7 8 9   (p. 30)
(Circle One)

Which Level is it?  First / Second / Third  (p. 30)
(Circle one)

Notes on the Numerical value:  (p. 33-39)

Notes on the Level:  (p. 30-31)

Notes on the Position:  (p. 44-50)

## Special considerations:

Notes on any double letters. Vowels or consonants? (p. 51)


Notes on any 'th' or 'ie' combinations.  (p. 50)



Pivot letter(s)  _____  (p. 46)

(This will be one or two center letters)

*The pivot letter(s) are how the person needs to interact with others to be able to fulfill their life's purpose*

Notes:


*These next letters show how you influence others and the ways you use your talents to interact with them*

The Letter on Left side of Pivot  (p. 48)  _____

Notes:



The Letter on Right side of Pivot  (p. 48)  _____

Notes:

Now combine all these clues using the key words you have noted. This will give you an excellent picture of your personality and insights into your hidden gifts and challenges.

Don't worry if you don't get every last detail of information. You will have gotten a great deal of new information as you worked through this book.

For additional work book pages go to:
*www.dollymae.com*.

For questions and consultations email
dolly@dollymae.com

In 1972 Dolly began building an extensive real estate enterprise. She bought and renovated hundreds of buildings, creating affordable housing. She operated a general contracting company and a property management team. Dolly trained thousands of people in the art of real estate acquisition, financing, and management.

A bank failed, her real estate empire collapsed, and she found herself in a $25 million bankruptcy. There was no way to go but up and she embarked on a quest to find meaning in what had happened. This process revealed her highly developed intuition.

Refining the techniques she used to bring herself back from the brink of disaster, she explains how to bounce back in her best selling book Choosing Joy in the Midst of Crisis.

One of the techniques she learned along the way involved using names and how to unmask the challenges and gifts in each one. Her book If You Have a Name, You Need This Book\* is the result of that information.

She conducts private consultations, seminars and workshops combining intuition and business worldwide. Her down-to-earth personality and forthright solutions to personal growth make her a popular speaker and frequent guest on TV and radio talk shows.

Dolly lives in the greater Seattle area and can be contacted through her website www.dollymae.com, by email at: dolly@dollymae.com or by phone 877.246.9569.